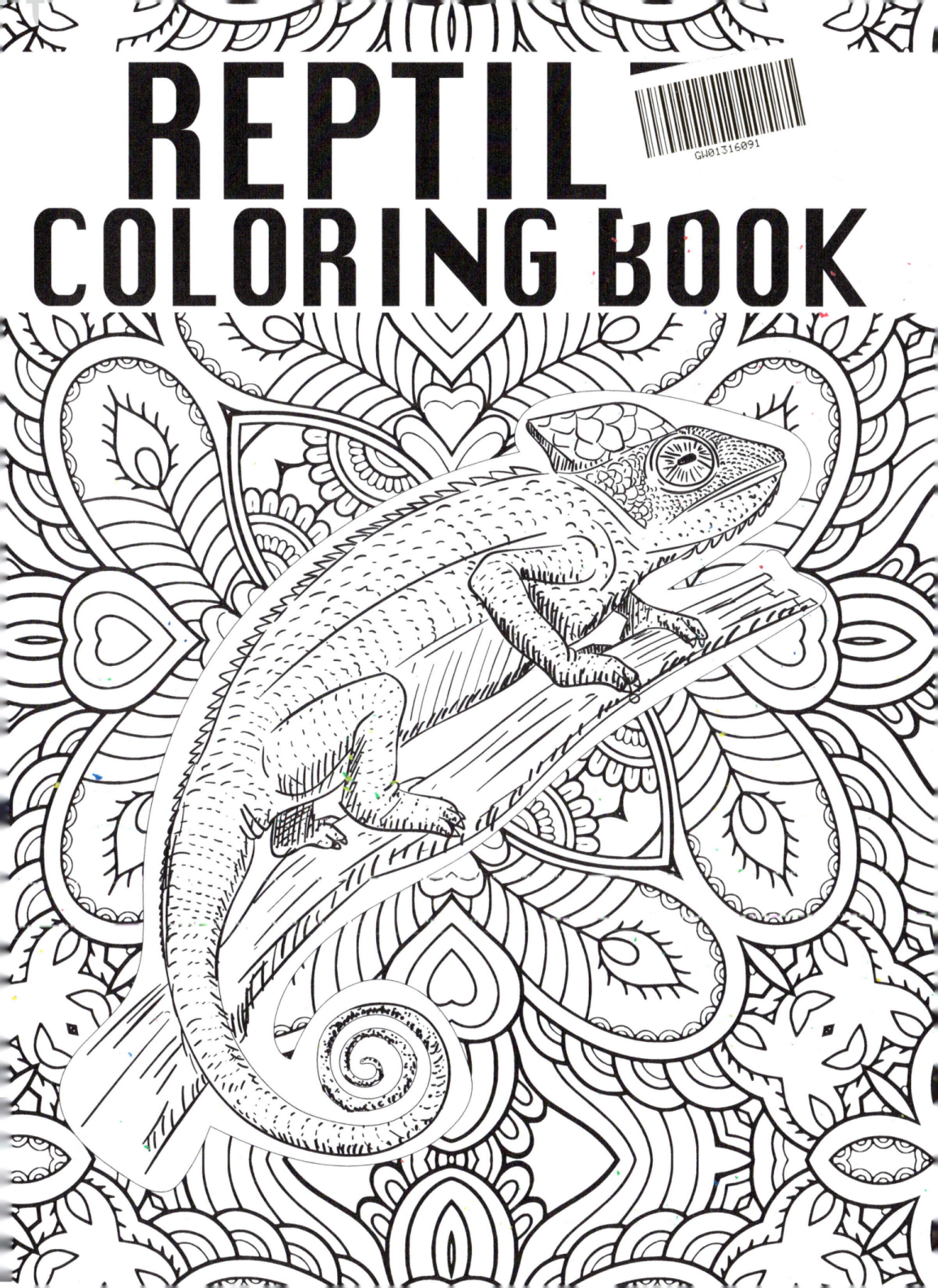

THIS BOOK BELONGS TO:

Copyright © 2021 Francisco W. Golden. All rights reserved.

No part of this publication may be reproduced, distributed, or transmitted in any form or by any means, including photocopying, recording, or other electronic or mechanical methods, without the prior written permission of the publisher, except in the case of brief quotations embodied in critical reviews and certain other noncommercial uses permitted by copyright law.

COLOR TEST PAGE

Go for it!

Printed in Great Britain
by Amazon